I Never Would Have Made It

ILA BOYD LOCKHART

CONTENTS

Preface	7
Dedications	9
Introduction	15

In-A-Box 17

Chapter 1: Mom Has Fallen for a Mask-Wearer	19

Grandma, Why Did You Go? 21

Chapter 2: Mom Goes to Church. Dad Becomes a Wolf	23
Chapter 3: The Demon in Him	25
Chapter 4: Hello, World! Here Comes Ila	27
Chapter 5: This Little Girl	29

$1.00 per Crime 31

Daddy, Stop Killing Us 33

Were You Blind? 35

There Was Nothing I Could Do 37

Chapter 6: There He Goes Drinking Again	39

You're Cutting My Heart 41

Chapter 7: Foster Care the First Time	43
Chapter 8: We Were Poor, But We Made It	45
Chapter 9: The Same Yesterday, Today, and Tomorrow	49
Chapter 10: Becoming the Person I Hated the Most	51
Chapter 11: My Rescuer	53
Chapter 12: My Angel	55

Where Will This White Girl Carry Me? 57

Meth – Life or Death 59

Chapter 13: The Worst I've Ever Been	61

I Bleed and I Bleed 63

Chapter 14: Why, God, Can't I Have a Baby?	65

My Baby's Waiting in Heaven 67

Goodbye, Sweetheart. I Never Heard You Call My Name 69

Chapter 15: My Dad and the KKK   71

Frozen for a Long Time 73

Chapter 16: All I Wanted Was Love   75

Chapter 17: I Became a Prostitute (Lot Lizard)   77

Chapter 18: Truly Knowing God   79

Chapter 19: Where I Met the Man I Married   81

Joy and Pain 83

Chapter 20: He Became My Baby   85

You Couldn't Break Me 87

In the Garden (Dirt) – A New Start 89

This Little Girl 91

Chapter 21: Letting Go   93

Good Little Girl in Me 97

My Father Said "No" 99

Chapter 22: The Man God Handpicked for Me   101

A Different Love 105

The Love That Taught Me Everything 107

Tears to Laughter 109

How Your Love Feels 111

Then to Now 113

New Attitude 115

Afterword: I Surrender All (will you?)   117

But God 119

There is help...   121

There is hope...   123

Preface

If I know anything at all, I know God has called me to write this book to help others who have struggled with sexual, mental, physical, and verbal abuse. Such abuse comes in many forms and fashions, from many different types of people. The pain inflicted is indescribable.

If you are in the grips of pain or abuse, present or past, I want to tell you what I have learned. You don't have to be afraid anymore. You don't have to be ashamed. It's not your fault, and it never was. You must face your fear, and you must forgive all those who have trespassed against you. Yes, you must forgive everyone who has wronged you. Does this mean you have to see them again face to face? No, but you do have to forgive them.

Jesus, in Matthew 6:14, says, "If you forgive men for their trespasses, your heavenly Father will also forgive you." Forgiveness means you are willing to make a change. Forgiving means that you're not like them. It means that they did not break you. Forgiveness makes you stronger than they are. When you forgive, they cannot hurt you anymore. They lose control.

People in my life I have forgiven: my dad, my mom, my sisters, my friends, my ex-husbands, the members of the KKK. Anyone else I might have forgotten, I forgive all of you.

God, help me to let go of all the bitterness and resentment. You are the One who binds up and heals the brokenhearted. I receive Your anointing that breaks and destroys every yoke of bondage. I receive emotional healing by faith, according to Your Word: "And with his stripes we are healed" (Isaiah 53:5). I thank You for giving me the grace to stand firm until the process is complete. Thank You for being my wise counselor. I acknowledge the Holy Spirit as my wonderful counselor! Thank You for helping me work out my salvation with fear and trembling, for it is You, Father, who works in me to will and act according to Your good purpose. In the name of Jesus, I choose to forgive those who have wronged me. I choose to live my life in forgiveness because You have forgiven me. With the help of the Holy Spirit, I get rid of all resentment, bitterness, rage, anger, brawling, and slander, along with every form of malice. I desire to be kind and compassionate to others, forgiving them just as Christ has forgiven me. Amen.

The Bible tells us that forgiveness is a two-way street. We must forgive, but we must also seek forgiveness. As I forgive those who have hurt me, there are many of whom I need to ask forgiveness. I need to be honest about the exact nature of my wrongs. I have to ask God to forgive me. When possible, I need to make amends to those I have wronged. When I ask for forgiveness, I am forgiven. Then I am set free to forgive others.

I choose to walk in forgiveness.

Dedications

First and foremost, I thank You, God. Without You I never would have made it, would never have found You. I thank You for all the dear people You have put in my life. Thank You for helping me grow from a hurt, confused little girl into a blessed, highly favored woman of God, grateful to be alive.

Leron Lockhart. Other than God, there's nobody greater to me. You, now and always, will be first in my life. I love you with everything in me. You are my husband, my soulmate, my best friend. You have heard the good, the bad, and the ugly of my life, and you are still here. You are the first man in my life who didn't want to use me. You taught me how to trust, how to slow down, how to be loved and how to love. I know without a doubt that you adore me. I see it in your eyes. I feel it in your touch. You give me courage and confidence. You believe in me. God handpicked you just for me to love all my pain away.

To the man and woman who made God's Word come alive in me – Doctor (Pastor) Ronald D. Sterling and First Lady Kim Sterling of Birmingham, Alabama. I love you both so much. There is no possible way I could ever forget you, especially the way you share with and listen to people who are hurting. You are the strongest people I know. I can only pray to be as humble and compassionate as you. Pastor, a special thanks to you for being a man of God. You are humble, never taking credit for anything, saying it's not you but God who lives in you. I have never met anyone with so much faith, trusting God for everything. You introduced me to God in a way that changed my life forever. Because of you, I know how valuable I am. I am rich, a daughter of the King. You and Kim will always be my spiritual dad and mom, and I will always be your little white sheep.

Doctor John Crider, thank you and Donna for everything you have done. I will never forget you. Doctor Randy Stewart, thank you for always listening to me and helping me when I needed it. All three of you encouraged me to keep going, to believe that I could do anything I put my mind to doing.

Wayne Sellers, you are a great man. I met you when I was very young in foster care. You were the head of DHR. You showed me such kindness, and always with a smile. You told me, "Miss Ila, you are very smart, and you should do something with your talents. You don't have to be a nobody just because people say you're a nobody." If in life we could choose our own dads, I would have chosen you. Thank you for everything.

Brother Steven Schmidt, the man who wouldn't stop showing up at the right time. You never stopped knocking on my door. Every Saturday you would come and say, "I'll be here in the morning if you want to go to church." You knew we were using drugs, but you still kept coming every Saturday. I want to thank you for never giving up on me. I used to read my poems to you, and you said that one day these poems would be my message. You were right. God took my mess and turned it into His message. After you heard my testimony, you told me, "It's an honor to know you." No one had ever told me that before. Thank you!

Mother, without you I would not be here, and without your prayers I never would have made it. I told you once that I hated you, because I felt you knew what my dad was doing to me. But you said you didn't know. I love you! Mostly on your own, you bore and raised six girls. You lived in as much hell as we did. If you had not been a Christian and prayed all those prayers, we would all be dead. Thank you for loving God... and me.

Paula Joslin, a lady who is really an angel, an earth angel. She's in a group called the B-Team Angels that goes to hospitals, churches, and other places in God's name. She saw something good in me. She asked and encouraged me to write this book and share my life, so that I might help others to overcome and be the best they can be. She told me that it's never too late to change, that God can do anything except fail. She reminded me that God loves me so much that He gave His only Son Jesus to die so that I might live. Thank you, angel Paula.

You all have inspired me to believe in myself and to know that *I'm worth it!* Without you, I never would have made it. A big "thank you" to all of you.

I consist of a delightful blend of six beautiful ladies.

I am the fourth, and I was also the most daring.

I always had to learn the hard way (my way).

Don't cry for me.

I live to tell it.

Introduction

In my distress I cried to the Lord, and He heard me.
Psalm 120:1

I have been hurt deeply by the people in my life I love the most. Along the way, I have hurt myself deeply, too. I have been emotionally unstable for most of my life, in every jail within a hundred mile radius. At times writing would calm me, but at other times it would do just the opposite.

Without God and the people He has placed in my life, I never would have made it. I am now a believer. I don't judge others, criticize, or gossip. I now believe God should be my only focus, my only program. I know that I am only human and that I am not perfect, but I strive to be.

I was told by my sister-in-law that my late mother-in-law, Grace Lockhart, often said, "If you're going to worry, don't pray. But if you're going to pray, don't worry." I once was controlled by worry; now I choose to pray.

My name is Ila Boyd Lockhart. As you start to read my story, you might say, "Not another book about someone's life!" You might think it's just the same old story, of no benefit to anyone. Hopefully, that's not true. Sometimes, people's lives are changed by hearing what others have endured and overcome.

So why not kick off your shoes, get something to drink, and relax? Let's take a journey together. Forget about reality TV. Tune in to my life. It's full of liars, thieves, cursing, life and death, love and hate, drama, rape, jail time, and abuse. It begins with a frightened little girl and her sisters, beaten and hiding. It ends with courage and strength straight from a loving God.

God, I pray that You write for me, that the memories are all true and not falsified. I thank You for the courage to do this. I pray no one gets hurt as the truth is told. All of this is written in hopes of helping others, young and old, garner the same courage You gave me. I pray for healing of the mind and heart of every one who reads this book. Amen.

I think we should stop letting people program us, speaking negatively about us, always telling us that we're nothing and will always be nothing. Instead, we should start letting God program us. He will renew our minds and release our inner "butterfly". In a lot of ways, we start life in a cocoon, trapped by people who put us down. But when God takes over, He releases us and gives us wings to fly. He transforms us into beautiful creatures. No one can put us back into the cocoon but ourselves.

As my story unfolds, you will see a miraculous metamorphosis, engineered by God. To Him be the glory forever and ever!

IN-A-BOX

Close me in a box.
Close the lid up tight.
I don't need to see.
I don't need the light.

Close me in a box.
Close the lid up tight.
I won't even struggle.
I won't even fight.

Close me in a box.
Close the lid up tight.
I can't really breathe,
But that's still alright.

Close me in a box.
Close the lid up tight.
You'll never take my soul,
Be it day or night.

Close me in a box.
Close the lid up tight.
You'll never break my spirit,
And I'll never stop the fight.

So squeeze me all you wish.
Try to put me in the wrong.
From the outside I look weak,
But on the inside I am strong.

Chapter One

Mom Has Fallen for a Mask-Wearer

On September 29, 1934 my dad was born to William Glen Boyd and Ila Route Boyd in Sylacauga, Alabama. My dad grew up in poverty and brutality. Grandad was, in every sense of the word, a mean man. In contrast, Grandma was the sweetest woman I have ever known. I don't know all that my dad went through growing up, but it probably contributed to his later role as an abuser.

My mother was born to Oscar Clarence Bailey and Beatrice Alma Bailey on November 23, 1941 in Tapan, West Virginia. Her dad was a drunkard who worked in the coal mines, and her mother was a stay-at-home wife. They were poor but prideful people who managed to provide the essentials to their children.

Neither my parents nor grandparents were saved until later in life. Their personal histories reflected this. By the time my dad and mom met, she had three children from two previous marriages. My dad put on the mask of a loving man, and she fell for it. She wasn't saved then, so they would go to bars and drink. He was a charmer, and she fell madly in love with him. His good looks reminded her of actor James Garner on *Maverick*. She was blinded by love and could not see the real Roy Boyd – the alcoholic, the beater, the rapist, the child molester, and (oh yes, let's not forget) the church man. He told her he wanted to marry her, to be a good dad and provide for her kids, and she fell in love with the man and his promises.

When my older sister, Lisa, heard that Mom was getting married, she was so excited. She wanted so much to have a father-daughter relationship. She talked about being a good girl, getting his coffee and slippers, and making him proud of her.

So they married, and immediately the foundation of his promises to Mom began to crumble. And the wonderful father-daughter relationship that Lisa longed for turned into something opposite... a nightmare.

Grandma, Why Did You Go?

Grandma, I miss you so.
I need to know if you're ok.
I didn't get a chance to ask before you had to go.
Why was my daddy so mean to you and me?

Why did you have to leave me?
I was so scared; now I'm grown and still need you.
Are you ok?
Can't you send me a sign to ease my mind?

I tried to come where you are,
but God said it wasn't my time to go.
He needs me to tell the things of my past
so someone can be saved.

So Grandma, stop fussing.
I'll be there soon.
It's Ila, your little raccoon.

Chapter Two

Mom Goes to Church
Dad Becomes a Wolf

Not long after Mom and Dad were married, she started going to church, found God, and began living for Him. She quit drinking and going out. My dad hated that. He started drinking more and more. He would sometimes disappear for days with Mom not knowing where he was, not knowing whether he was dead or alive. She caught him in an extramarital relationship with her sister and forgave him, but he did it again. Then he started beating her, accusing her of cheating on him. (You've heard the old saying, "A guilty dog will bark.") She'd find jobs to feed us, but he'd get drunk and take her money. He became another man, an abusive man. Cursing and beating became a daily occurrence at breakfast, dinner, and supper.

Despite all this, Mom would not leave him because, like most abused women, she prayed he would change and because she found out she was pregnant with me. But he just got meaner and meaner. He would fight with anyone at any time. Once he brutally beat Risa and Nancy's dad who had come unannounced to see them. He would steal from people and then return the stolen items, trying to sell them back with a smile on his face. Nothing seemed to get better for Mom. The more she tried, the worse he became. He was in and out of jail all of the time. It probably would have been better for all of us if he had stayed there.

Chapter Three

The Demon in Him

My mom was in bed with a "migraine" after being beaten. Dad told two of my sisters to stay outside. If they tried to come in, he threatened to kill them. One was seven years old, the other six years old. Then he took Lisa, my oldest sister, into the house and raped her. She was only eight years old. He told her that if she let anyone know, he would never stop tormenting her. If she kept quiet, she would be his favorite.

Lisa did not tell anyone for about five months. All the while, my dad kept on raping her because he knew he could get away with it. He knew she was not going to tell.

I'm going to jump ahead a bit. After we were all grown up, Lisa told me about the sexual abuse. She said that she was terrified of Dad and had recurring dreams of not being able to get away from him. No matter where she would hide, he would find her. This has affected her entire adult life and ruined her first marriage.

Now back to her childhood. Lisa finally got the courage to tell Mom what he was doing to her. Mom was pregnant with me at the time, and Dad had beaten her so badly this time that she went into labor. The police had to be called, and Dad was taken into custody. It was while he was away that Lisa told Mom about Dad's actions.

The court proceeding took place on July 27, 1973. My dad spoke to the judge. "Your honor, may I have a word with my daughter?" The judge said "yes," but Lisa would not go to him.

The judge then told him, "You can say what you have to say to her from there."

"Honey," Dad said to Lisa, "if Daddy's done to you what you accused him of, will you forgive him?"

The judge sentenced him to eight months in prison, but it was reduced to probation only. He never served any jail time. The judge also spoke with Lisa in his chambers and asked her what Dad did to her. I will not tell you all he did, but the acts she described were so ungodly and horrible that the judge cried, saying no one should ever have to endure what she had been through.

Close your eyes and think about an eight-year-old girl, a grown man, and a screw driver. Enough said.

Chapter Four

Hello, World! Here comes Ila.

I was born August 2, 1968 in Huntington, West Virginia, two months premature and weighing 3 pounds and 2 ounces. I had no fingernails, no toenails, and no hair. My lungs were not developed, and I had severe head pain stemming from Dad's beatings while Mom was pregnant with me. I was so very tiny. I would cry a lot, and my Dad would scream at me because of the crying. Again resorting to abuse, he burst my eardrums and then refused to let the doctor put tubes in my ears.

I would gain a pound and lose a pound, until a nurse at the hospital told my mom to take me up into the mountains to see an old man. He put me on goat's milk, and that did the trick.

Isaiah 44:2 – "I am your Creator. You were in My care before you were born."

I still cried a lot, however. Even several shots in my head from the doctor didn't work. So Dad decided to put beer in my bottles to make me pass out. I had been born early because of his beatings. Now he was tormenting me out of the womb. He was a sick drunk with many, many demons. He would beat Mom just for praying. Sometimes she had to sneak us out of the house so we could go to church, even though she knew the consequences when she would return home. She said it was worth the risk to have her babies hear the Word of God.

My mom eventually left him, but he kept finding us and kept beating us. When we went to the house of my mom's brother to hide, Dad found us and dragged Mom back home by the hair. Then he beat us with a leather razor strap, warning us, "If your sorry Mama wants to leave, you better not go with her no more."

My sisters and I started praying, "God, You said, 'Ask, believe, and receive.'" That's all we knew to do. But there seemed to be no answer from Heaven. Daddy just got meaner and meaner from that day forward.

Chapter Five

This Little Girl

The sexual abuse continued, and now he included me as his victim. It began when I was only three years old and lasted for years. Night after night we sisters would cry ourselves to sleep and hold each other tight, because we never knew whom he was coming for.

Then we found out that Mom was pregnant with my sister Agnes. She was born in Sylacauga, Alabama on June 1, 1971. Because of this, things quieted down for a little while.

My older sister said that the only time she could remember being happy was when Dad was going to church. We went to church as a happy family (in appearance only). Dad made all the church people think he was a good man, but he was just the opposite. At night he would leave a dollar under our pillow so we would not say anything about what he was doing to us.

I was just six years old, but I really wanted to die. He hurt us so much that I'd jump if he even moved a finger in my direction. I would stay as much as possible at the house of Red and Bissie Andrews, parents of one of my sister's friends. They were good to us, and they loved us. They never called me Ila; instead, they called me Bambie.

Then, alas, Mom became pregnant again, for the last time. (I think DHR made her get her tubes tied.) My baby sister was about to be born.

$1.00 per Crime

Each time you came for one of us you left a dollar behind,
as if to say you paid for the time
it took for you to commit the crime
upon your own little girls and your step-daughter too.
Was my mom not enough for you?
Or were you so greedy you had to have her children too?
They shouldn't call you a man.
You're an animal; you should live at the zoo.

Why did you do what you did and ask us not to tell?
I hope you ask God to forgive you.
If not, then right now you're in Hell.
(As a matter of fact, you left us Hell.)
We're all grown now.
Lisa has been tormented by you in her dreams all her life.
Don't you think it's time to release us
from your spell so we can grow?

I forgive you, Daddy.
Leave us, and leave us alone.

Daddy, Stop Killing Us

My heart died when I was three years old.
My childhood was stolen,
and I never had a say in it.

I became unwanted and unloved by the people I love the most.
I was fighting like a grown woman
and crying like a little girl.
Most kids were playing and laughing,
but I couldn't even smile.

It was our secret,
and no one else should know.
A dollar under my pillow and a kiss on my forehead,
a smile and a wink,
diabolical words coming from my real Dad.
That's the first time I wished I was dead.

Over the next four years I cried myself to sleep each night.
He never held me like his little girl.
He used me.
I tried to put this in the back of my mind.
I would ask God, "Why?"
I would ask Him to let me die.

I tried so hard to be a good girl,
thinking he would love like a daddy should.
Instead I grew up scared to love.
I would lay there and think,
"This can't be love."

Were You Blind?

Each time you saw me...
Could you not see my anger?
Could you not see my hurt
from all the dirty things
you did and made me do?

Every day of my life you were killing me.
The little girl in me you made into a whore.
I can't bear any children because of you.

I have to know...
Did you fulfill your need
before or after you made me bleed?
You climbed on top of me like a snake.

Did I do something wrong, Daddy?
When you looked at me,
didn't you see your little girl?
Didn't you see *me*?

There Was Nothing I Could Do

Oh, little sis, is that really you
who came into the world
all battered and bruised?

I said I'd take care of you
whenever he'd come for you.
I'd take your place.

I couldn't stand the thought
of him hurting you again.
I tried to make it better
by trying to make you laugh.
But he'd always make us cry.

If I could have ever stopped the pain,
I would have done it for you.
I'm sorry, little sister.
I couldn't make it stop.

He looked at us in lust, not out of love.
I'm sorry, little sister.
He finally got you too.

This makes me angry.
There was nothing I could do
but hold your little body
when he was through.

Chapter Six

There He Goes Drinking Again

Whenever Roy Boyd would start drinking, my mom would go into the closet to cry and pray, because she knew the beatings would come. By now, we were on welfare and food stamps. Dad was no longer working.

One of my few good childhood memories is of a chicken house behind our residence that had not been used in years. We girls would carry Mama's old furniture down there and build playhouses. Each of us constructed our own playhouse, often with boards and buckets for furniture. We would go and "visit" each other, the rule being that we had to knock on the door before coming in. If I barged in without knocking, Risa would push me out of her house. I'd get up and do it again, and she'd push me out a second time. My sister Lisa even threw a bucket of water on me when I entered her house unannounced. Sometimes I would pretend to call Lisa on the phone and ask her permission to come over. We had so much fun in that imaginary world.

Reality was not any fun at all. My mom and dad got a divorce, and the tug-of-war for us began. One day Dad tricked us into getting into a car with him, telling us that we were playing a joke on Mom. He kidnapped us and took us to his mother's house in Sylacauga. Grandma scolded him and pleaded with him to return us home. During the night he even stole money from her, his own mother. The next morning five police cars pulled up. They put Dad in one car and us in the others. Dad went to prison; we went back home.

When Dad got out of prison, he came to our school and got us again. He took us to Talladega to a hotel. I was seven years old, my younger sister was five, and little Bea was only six months old. He left all of us there alone for hours. My sisters were crying because they were hungry, and I did everything I knew to do (rocking, singing, playing. etc.), but nothing made them stop.

After a night and a day, I finally went for help. There was a black lady in the restaurant who was breastfeeding her baby, and I asked her if she could come help my baby sister stop crying. She said, "Honey, where's your mom and dad?" I didn't want to get my dad in trouble, so I started to leave. But she came with me anyway and saw my sisters crying. She fed Bea, and I told her what my daddy had done. Because my older sister Lisa had just taught me how to sing my telephone number, the lady was able to call my mom and the local police.

Back at home, I said, "Mama, I did a good job!" But she replied, "Why do you keep leaving with him?" I was hoping to get a hug or something.

You're Cutting My Heart

I tried and tried.
I cried and cried.
Why am I so sensitive to others?
Can't they see how much they are hurting me?

Am I not here?
Hello! Can anybody hear me?
What's wrong with me?
Why can't anyone see me?

I've searched and searched inside and out of me.
Maybe it's just not meant to be.
I have too much love, but how can that be?
Am I smothering you?
Or maybe I don't love *me*.

I'm not blind.
Why can't I see?
I have a voice, but I cannot speak.
I have a heart, but I cannot feel.
Why?

Chapter Seven

Foster Care the First Time

I was placed in foster care. Gail Cagle was my foster mom. She had a daughter named Marie and a lot of foster kids, so we never got lonely. When I arrived there, she bought me some blue jeans. Since I had never worn pants before, I thought this was cool.

Gail was always good to us and never treated us differently than her own daughter. She took us on vacation to Opryland every year. If my grades were bad, she would not whip me. Instead, she would take away something that meant a lot to me, like dessert or TV.

She gave us an allowance, but if we left the light on she would take a quarter away. She taught us a lot of good things: how to be independent and how to work hard. We would work in the big garden, in the hayfields, and in the house. We washed walls and made our own beds.

She also taught us to be responsible. If we turned it on, we were to turn it off. If we opened it, we must close it. If we got it dirty, we should clean it.

And she lived what she taught. She was not lazy at all. That woman would work from daylight to dark.

Chapter Eight

We Were Poor, But We Made it

Back at home and out of foster care, our life was marked by poverty. Mom tried hard to put food on the table, often crying out to God for help and strength. I remember once, when Mom was praying, that there was a knock on the door. A young couple had come with a gift of food. They said that they were shopping and felt led to fill their buggies with food for someone else. Somehow God led them to our house with a carload of food! Mom just started praising God for His blessings.

I remember once, when a storm was coming, that my mom started praying. Everything to the right and left of our house was damaged, but our house was spared. (Isn't God wonderful?)

In all of the sadness we endured, I always tried to be the funny one. I saw how my mom and sisters wept a lot, so I tried to make them laugh to keep them from crying. I'd tell people we were so poor that Mom would feed us three meals each day: oatmeal, no meal, and miss a meal. I would rearrange the name of food so it wouldn't sound the same: "Tonight we're having beans and taters. Tomorrow we're having taters and beans." I also told people we were so poor that Mom put two of us in the same diaper just to get ends to meet. I would joke that normal people took bubble baths, but we took baths in dish soap and came out of the tub smelling like a plate.

It wouldn't be wrong to say I was also mean and sneaky. My mom put me in timeout in the bathroom, but this didn't work because I got in the tub and took a bath. The next time she put me in a chair facing the wall, and I pulled all the paper off the wall. I think I had ADD, or perhaps it was just meanness. She would accuse me of defending my dad, and I would say, "I hate you, and I love my daddy." But I did love her very much.

When we got in trouble as a group, my mom would put us all on the floor on a blanket and try to get us to sleep by using a slow, monotone voice. She would say, "You're walking in the green, green grass. It's so smooth and looks like velvet. You can see a big mansion on the hill." Everyone would almost be asleep, and I'd raise my leg up in the air and make a noise with my mouth. Everyone would jump up and holler.

My sisters, Lisa and Risa, would make me stand like a dummy holding the antenna in place so they could watch TV. They would tell me what a good job I was doing, and they would be laughing at me the whole time. They would also make me pop the popcorn and then tell me, "Nobody pops it like you, Ila." They had a lot of fun at my expense.

All of us had fun at Mom's expense. She was kindhearted, letting us have slumber parties every Saturday night so she could take all the kids to church on Sunday. But she also had a vain streak. She entered almost every sweepstakes, and she was always hoping she would be the next million dollar winner.

One day we arranged for one of our older male cousins to call her and say that she had won the sweepstakes. Mom started running back and forth, praising God, saying, "I'm gonna pay my tithes and buy a new car. What do you kids want?" All of a sudden it wasn't so funny to us, and we felt badly when we had to tell her the truth. She didn't whip us, but it felt like she did. Although we didn't intend to do so, we hurt her.

As I got older, I would hurt her over and over again, although deep down I really didn't want to do so. I became more rebellious.

Chapter Nine

The Same Yesterday, Today, and Tomorrow

My mom wasn't the only one in need. So was I. And just like He did with her, God took care of me. I remember being so hungry one day that I got on my knees and cried out to God: "God, I'm hungry. You told me that You would take of me if I'd ask."

Before thirty minutes had passed, my neighbor knocked on the door and said, "Miss Ila, would it hurt your feelings if we gave you some food. We had a family reunion and had some food left over."

I said, "No, ma'am," and went outside with her. They had brought me a whole truckload of food.

Thirty-eight years later a tornado swept through my hometown of Arab, Alabama. As destruction was happening all around me, I slept through it like a baby. I was awakened by my niece Amber, screaming and crying, "Aunt Ila, get up! Don't you know what's happened? Arab is gone. It's destroyed."

During the next few minutes, a friend of mine took a picture of the damage near my trailer. The photo showed something that was absolutely amazing. Trees were uprooted, and my underpinning was gone. But Jesus could be seen in the picture, standing there with both hands on top of the trailer, as if he were holding it down.

God is good... yesterday, today, and tomorrow.

Chapter Ten

Becoming the Person I Hated the Most

After three years in foster care, I came back home. I started feeling resentment towards my mom for everything, so I became rebellious. I started hanging out with my sister's friend Susan, a "wild child". I liked her. We would smoke pot and drink. I discovered this would make the pain of the past go away, at least for a while, so I drank more.

We were the life of the party. If Ila was there, you were guaranteed to have a good time. I liked being the center of attention, and I loved being loved by those around me. If you weren't partying with me, you weren't partying. All night long I'd fight and steal, get high, and party all over again. I would sleep with this one then that one – fat, skinny, black, white, short, tall. I had no preference, as long as I could get drunk and high to block out all the pain. If I dated someone, he would most often be at least ten to twenty years older than me.

See the pattern? My behavior was just like my dad's. I was becoming the man I hated the most. How could this be? I despised him.

It was about this time that my mom stopped going to church. She met a young Hispanic man, about twenty-five years old, named Pedro. They had a brief relationship, but Mom ended it. Next she met an older man named Layon Sterling, a brick mason who had his own business. He enticed Mom to drink and smoke. She drank Sterling beer because his name was on it and smoked Viceroy cigarettes because my dad's name was Roy.

During this time we were under a court order to see a psychiatrist. She prescribed us Elavil, an anti-depressant. She also told us that when a child is molested, he or she usually grows up to be a molester. She predicted I would someday mistreat or molest a child. But I looked her in the eye and said, "Lady, I don't believe that, because I have never, nor will I ever molest a child!" Then I walked out of the room.

I never did abuse a child in any way. But I continued to abuse my own body, this time with alcohol. I started drinking straight gin. I would go to bed with a bottle and get up with a bottle. I lived with my mom and worked the third shift at Dana in Arab. My boss and I would often go downstairs and drink during our breaks.

All this drinking around the kids prompted my mom to order me to leave the house by the end of the week. When that day came and I was still there, she took the girls and left herself.

Chapter Eleven

My Rescuer

After Mom left me, my friend would come every night when I got off work, and we would drink and get drunk. Sexual looseness continued as well. I would tell people that I was either from the "show me" state or the "try me" state.

Susan and I spent a lot of time partying in New Hope, Alabama. I started dating a guy named Tony Lipscomb who was of mixed race. Not long afterwards, I was kidnapped by two men as I was walking home. They threw me into their van, raped me, and hurled racial insults at me. "If you can go with a nigger," they said, "you can go with us."

After three days of abuse, sexual and physical, they threw me out of the van. A local police officer noticed me and carried me to the ER.

When the two brothers heard that I had filed a police report, they came and got me again. They took me to an old house and abused me again for five days.

Susan learned where I was and saved me. She crashed her car into the house, picked me up in her arms, and threatened the men with a gun. Then she took me back to the hospital to be evaluated again. I was admitted and stayed there two weeks. I was so badly injured that the doctor said I might never walk again.

But God had other plans.

Chapter Twelve

My Angel

After I mended, I started hanging out with the wrong crowd again. One night I went to a dance in Ruth and was drinking with a guy. I asked him to give me a ride to my mom's house, and he agreed, but about halfway home he told me to get out of his car.

As I began to walk toward home, a car drove by and stopped. The driver was calling out a girl's name. He offered me a ride home, and I accepted his invitation. During the ride, he shared his story. He told he was looking for his daughter. He said she had called and told him that she was walking and needed a ride home.

I got out of the car in my mom's driveway and turned around to say "thank you" to the man. But he was not there anymore. My mom told me he was my angel.

Unfortunately, I still wanted to get high. There seemed to be radar inside of me when it came to finding drugs and no-good men. I wanted so badly to be loved, and I would fall for their lies when they said they loved me. In a few days, however, they would be beating me. I tried to smile on the outside, but I was always crying on the inside. I didn't realize that each time I slept with a man I was slowly dying, killing a piece of me.

One night, while I was "pilled up", I went to sleep in a tanning bed and suffered second and third degree burns all

over my body. My corneas were burned, and there was fear
that I would lose my sight. Once again, God had other plans.

Where Will This White Girl Carry Me?

I'm acing.
I'm not faking.
Crying inside, laughing outside,
so confused, drained, no energy.
Constant thoughts fill my mind,
driving me crazy. I am insane.
Where have I been? Is it too late?
Is this world I live in about to come to an end?
Do I have time to make amends?
Where are all my friends?

Release me and let me go.
Don't come around here anymore.
I hide my face in shame,
only myself to blame.
You say all I write is lame,
but let me tell you,
Crystal meth is no game.
She'll rule you and take your soul,
steal your beauty, make you unrecognizable;
Your mind she will control.
She'll make you do whatever she pleases –
lying, cheating, stealing, killing.

When will this madness stop?
Will I make it to the top?
Imagine if I died.
Make it stop!

It's all echoing in my head:
"Get a gun filled with lead.
Pull the trigger."
Bang! I'm dead.
She would not have it any other way.
She would not have settled for less.
You will have to read my obituary:
"Another claimed by meth,
brought to her death, a sad refrain."

Now she's searching for new souls, young and old.
She doesn't discriminate on whom to take,
destroying everybody, you and I.
She dishes out hate after hate.
Don't look at her!
She will destroy you and everything you love.
You do the math:
Freedom or death on meth.
She alienates you one puff at a time.
A few more puffs, and you'll be gone.
Crystal meth, she will linger on.

Meth – Life or Death

Do you see what I see?
I'm looking in the mirror,
but who's that looking back at me?
That can't be me.
Am I sure that's who I see?
I guess it is me.

What happened to me?
Can someone tell me?
Where's my beauty?
I am unrecognizable.
A single tear runs down my face
as I notice the weight I've lost.
My smile is gone.

Who is this that's killing me?
Let me see my murderer.
What did I ever do to her to get on her hit list?
She's sucking the life out of me.
Can't you just let me be?
Is there nothing I can say?
Can I not make a plea for you to set me free?

Death becomes so real.
Don't they make a pill for this?
I was just smoking and toking, easing my mind.
Did I not see the signs?
Did I not hear her say, "You're mine"?

All this in my head:
"In a little while you'll be dead,
and meth will linger on."
I didn't know I was being led.
Get a gun and put it to my head.
Enough said!
Engrave my tombstone, 'cause I am dead.

Crystal meth is not your friend,
but she will be with you to the end,
Saying, "Look at you, fool!
I'm the one that killed you.
I've got to look around for my next victim.
My name is meth.
Some say I'm the best.
If you don't believe me, just keep smoking ice,
and you will see if your friend is nice."

So puff, puff, puff, puff on crystal meth.
Puff, puff, puff yourself to death.

Chapter Thirteen

The Worst I've Ever Been

I moved to Guntersville, Alabama. I was there about four weeks when I met Frank Moore, and he moved in with me. He and I started out great, like most relationships, but after four months his true colors started to show. We would get high, and he would start cursing and fighting me. Then he would want to go to bed with me.

I felt lower than dirt. I would lay there and cry all night. In the morning he would act like nothing happened. I almost hated him, but I could not make myself hate, even when he started beating me and threatening to kill my mother if I left him. I took many beatings from him I did not deserve.

I began planning a way out, but I needed money to do so. I started acting loving and romantic toward him to gain his trust, and he let me get a job babysitting for six months. While there, I stole the lady's diamonds, worth twenty thousand dollars. I did find a way out, at least for a while. I was arrested, went to jail, and did my time.

One night after I came home, Frank came home and accused me of letting a man out the back door. He beat me, stomped me with his feet, pulled my hair out, and kept kicking me. It took his brother and two friends to get him off of me. I lay on the couch for three days, my head pounding, I was not able to sleep or eat.

My face and lips then began to swell, so I called an ambulance. The paramedics notified my mom, and she came to help me. She didn't recognize me at first, because I was so disfigured, but she knew my voice.

When I looked in the mirror and saw myself, I really did not know if I was going to live or die. I cried out to God. I told Him that if He let me live, I'd never go back to Frank, and I didn't. Instead, I went to Sylacauga. Not surprisingly, it was not long until I was with another man.

I Bleed and I Bleed

Remember my pain I blocked out.
The past is like cutting yourself with a knife,
And I bleed and I bleed each time
a memory comes back to me.

I bleed and I bleed.
I put on a bandage for each new memory.
But still I bleed and I bleed.

I try to stitch up each new cut
by trying to understand,
But still I bleed and I bleed.

How can I make the bleeding and the pain go away?
All these memories come back so fast,
And still I bleed and I bleed.

When all my blood is on the floor, I will be no more.
But for now I bleed and I bleed.
Not until I forgive will the bleeding stop.

Would I be able to forgive you and dig my way out?
The more I learn to laugh and love,
the faster I will heal.

When I learn to trust and love,
I know my wounds will disappear.
Then my bandages I can remove.

The scars I bear will always remind me that love is true.

Chapter Fourteen

Why, God, Can't I Have a Baby?

I moved in with a man named Harold Whetstone from Sylacauga who was living with his aunt. I should have known from day one that something was wrong. He was lazy and would not work. We would fight all day and all night.

Things got even worse when we moved from his aunt's house to a trailer on his mother's property. There were no windows and no door. He became very jealous and controlling. I had to keep my head down whenever we were around any men. If I as much glanced at a man, he would tell them to leave, and he would beat me till blood was coming from my nose and ears.

I was so furious at him that I would not let him touch me. So he put scissors to my neck, climbed on top of me, and told me not to move. I lay there with tears rolling down my face.

During those days I began to feel a sick pain in stomach, and I began to vomit. So I went to a doctor and was told I was pregnant. I was so happy. I wanted so much to have a child I could love.

The pain continued, however. It was unbearable, and I was screaming and crying aloud. I went to the hospital, and before long they had me in surgery. I was pregnant in my tube, and the tube had burst and hemorrhaged. The doctor said I could have died.

Losing the pregnancy put me into a deep depression for months. I would just lay there in the bed crying for my baby.

After a few weeks I left Harold. My dad lived in Sylacauga, and I located him. I stayed at his house because I had nowhere else to go. I didn't want to go back to my mom as a failure once again.

The first night I was there he said, "Do you want to sleep with your daddy? You never get too old to sleep with your dad."

I said, "Let's get one thing straight. No, I won't sleep with you. I'm only here because I have nowhere to go."

With that understanding between us, I came and went to his house as I pleased.

My Baby's Waiting in Heaven

God looked down from heaven one afternoon.
He said,
"I need a flower in heaven to bloom.
He or she must be perfect in every way."

God reached out His hands and took my baby away.
My baby's in heaven by the Master's right hand.
Someday I'll join her or him in gloryland.

I woke up this morning with my heart filled with grief,
and God said, "Don't worry. Your baby's with me.
She or he is the most beautiful flower,
a lovely flower plucked from your home."

That flower will continue to bloom,
waiting for me,
until each other's face we finally see.

Goodbye, Sweetheart.
I Never Heard You Call My Name

Ode to the one who lived in me for such a short time.
I longed to hold you in my arm
and hear you say my name,
to watch you run and play,
to kiss you and say "I love you" each and every day.

Without a doubt your life would have been blessed.
Your mom would have given up all her crazy mess.

Since I was young I dreamed and prayed for you.
I even gave you a name.
If you were my little girl
your name was Erica Lasha,
and if you were my little boy your name was Joshua Miles.

I wanted so much to feel you live and breathe inside of me.
I imagine you were tiny and perfect with blue eyes like mine.

I knew you were special because you were mine.
But God needed you so much more.
I'll see you soon, my beloved.
With all my heart,
Mom

Chapter Fifteen

My Dad and the KKK

I met a guy named Mike, a black man, and we began seeing each other. One day, when he brought me home, my dad saw him (especially his color) and was very angry.

When I came home the next night, there was a chair in the middle of the kitchen, and Dad told me to have a seat. Then all of a sudden two men came into the room in KKK outfits. They beat me, urinated on me, and forced me to perform sexual favors. When they were finished, they left me there to die.

Mike couldn't get me to answer the phone, so he came and peeked through the back door and saw me. He carried me to the only place he could – a house that had been burned. We stayed in the living room section. He went and got Camels, food, blankets, pillows, and even some wood for a fire. He'd go to work and bring me food or whatever I needed every day.

I stayed there about a month, then I left Mike and went to my stepmom's house. There I met a guy named John Bone, and within fourteen days we were married. It was a huge mistake from the start. Within five months, he had run off with my younger stepsister. I tracked her down in Sylacauga and beat her, asking her where John was. She told me he was in Alexander City. She claimed he had left her for a man.

Frozen for a Long Time

Walking daily in a frozen zone;
it feels like someone is shooting ice water in my veins.
I can't find any warmth,
can't turn to my mother (she gave me away),
can't turn to my father (he raped me starting at age 3),
can't turn to my sisters (none of them are my friends).

I'm so alone, so lonely.
Sometimes I just stay in my room and cry.
I speak out loudly, very loudly, and no one hears.
I scream, and nobody hears.
My biggest fear is being left alone.

Where has everybody gone?
I can't move because I'm still frozen.
I've built a wall so tall and so wide.
They will never get to me in time.
Pain, hurt, disappointment, heartache, headache –
I'm broken, shattered to pieces.
Where's the glue?
I must be a fool to have ever believed love would find me.

It's freezing in here, and I can't feel anymore.
Lying on my bedroom floor,
I see shadows passing by my door.
I scream out once more,
"Hey, do you hear me? Hey, I'm here! Hey, hey, h-e-y!"
Nothing, no one.

I must do something with this ice;
then they will hear me and feel me.
Breathe, Ila, it's working! The ice is melting.
Breathe, breathe! Hurry before it's too late.
Faster, faster! Breathe!
Only I can save me.
Breathe!

Chapter Sixteen

All I Wanted Was Love

Let me remind you that I was only sixteen. At that young age I left with a girlfriend, Connie, hitchhiking to Florida. We caught a ride with a truck driver, a nice man who drove for a perfume company. He was good to us. When he stopped for a shower, he paid for us to get one too. He also gave us perfume and powder.

The truck driver had a big can full of quarters in his cab. When we got back into the truck, Connie got into it, and he caught her in the act. He put her out of the truck but allowed me to stay. He took me to a truck stop and got on his CB radio, asking if anyone was going towards Sylacauga. Eventually he found someone going to Montgomery, and he persuaded them to take me home. We had to wait three days, however, before leaving, because he was waiting for a load.

There were two other people in that truck, a black man and a black woman. They were running a business from inside that truck. The lady would get on the CB, talk to men, get out, and come back in about ten minutes with all kinds of money. Since I needed money for drugs at the time, I said to the driver, "Let me try."

He said, "Are you sure you want to be my girl?"

"What does that mean?" I replied.

"It means I get part of the money," he answered.

I said "okay" and asked the lady to teach me what to say and do to pick up a name. The first couple of times she went with me. I used the name Tamika. I figured if I could not find love, why not sell it?

Chapter Seventeen

I Became a Prostitute (Lot Lizard)

I made good money as a prostitute, mainly because I was white. It was a dangerous way to make a living. One day a man put a gun to my head, threatening me if I didn't do as he pleased. Out of nowhere another man came to my rescue and pointed a gun to his head, saying, "Let her go!." He did and then ran away. When I turned to thank my rescuer, he was gone. I think he was another angel watching over me.

God, do you love me that much, so much that You would keep saving this foolish girl?

One night I was with this little old man. He only had twenty-five dollars, but all he wanted to do was talk. His wife of sixty-three years had died, and he was looking for conversation. I sat and talked with him until he was finished. My pimp, Darrell, was not pleased. I tried to explain, but he slapped me and made me work overtime.

I would often tell my Johns (clients) that I was trying to get away. I'd charge a little more and put the excess in my sock, hoping to save enough to escape. One of the other girls told on me, and my pimp took the money and beat me.

A girl named Star also worked for him. Like all his girls, she got new clothes, an apartment, and money. One day she dropped a piece of paper in the trash and said, "Don't get it now." I waited thirty minutes before I retrieved it. I went to the store bathroom and read it: *If you're tired of being beat and want to look and smell like a lady and want money in your pocket, come see me. No harm will come to you. – Junkyard Dog*

Junkyard Dog's invitation was for me to leave my pimp Darrell and work for him In fact, the two men got into a bidding war for me. I was the only white girl out there, and I was a money-maker because that's what most Johns wanted. I was one of the top girls and got the best clothes, a nice apartment, and plenty of food. I only had to work four nights a week instead of seven.

Every day, however, I was trying to figure out how I could leave. Eventually I talked my pimp into letting me work a truck stop. I told a driver there what was happening, and he allowed me to crawl into the back of his truck and lie down. He drove me away and took me back to Sylacauga.

Chapter Eighteen

Truly Knowing God

After arriving in Sylacauga, it wasn't long before I moved to Birmingham. I stayed at the Salvation Army there. On Sundays we either had to be in the street all day or go to the Salvation Army church service. If we went, they would feed us afterwards.

My friends told me about a church they went to and about the great preacher there. They said they always went to Church's Chicken after the service, so I got on that van and went to church. All I went for was going out to eat. I did not have my mind focused on God, but little did I know that the short pastor was about to break me down on the inside. The preacher spoke straight from the Bible. He preached truth with such compassion and love for people. I adored him and his wife. They were the first people to ever show me real love.

So I began giving my life to the Lord. I wanted God to forgive me and change me. And He did. I was happy. I wasn't thinking about drugs, I wasn't in jail, and I wasn't thinking about a man.

The pastor told me to talk to God like I was talking to him. He said that I didn't have to beg God for anything, and it turned out he was right. I had a real one-on-one relationship with God. I would sing and talk to God all day, every day.

Chapter Nineteen

Where I Met the Man I Married

I went to the Jimmy Hale Mission one night. As I entered, a man standing there said, "When you get tired of playing with those little boys, come and holler at a man." I walked past him into the building every day for three weeks, and he would always say things like that to me.

One day I said, "Okay, John, take me to a dinner, a real dinner where you have to pay." He did, time and time again. He'd walk me to work and sit in the park with me.

He wanted us to go out together one Sunday, and I said, "No, but you can go to church with me." When he walked up to the shelter to get me, I was sitting on the steps, and he said I looked like an angel, the most beautiful thing he had ever seen. I fell into his trap.

Not long after, I stopped going to church because of him. He would accuse me of sleeping with the pastor, so I quit going altogether. It wasn't long before I was smoking crack again.

We decided that we weren't going to stay at the shelter anymore. We started sleeping under the 18th Street Bridge in Birmingham, along with about twenty other people. There was no privacy, so I took matters into my own hands. I found a big box behind a furniture store, placed it around my mattress, cut out two doors and a window, and made curtains and rods out of scratch material and coat hangers. *The Birmingham News* took pictures of my cardboard home.

We lived like this for about three months, then we went to an abandoned train. I said, "John, get a job, marry me, and put me in a house, or I'm leaving you. I'm tired, and I can do better than this myself." He did get a job, and we started staying in a motel. Eventually we were able to move into a house.

Yes, we did get married, and that's when everything started going wrong. The next twenty-one years of my life would be pure hell. John was verbally and physically abusive, always threatening to kill me. He also was unfaithful. I would sometimes invite girls from the shelter to spend the weekend, trying to show some love, and he would try to go to bed with them. He would steal money from me, and he would often hide things from me to try to make me think I was insane.

During our marriage, I started going back to church. He hated that. He would drink all the time, and I did everything I could to stay away from him. I even started selling and buying drugs, because I knew he would leave me alone if he had drugs at his side. I looked at him one night and saw an uncanny resemblance to my dad. The same demon now controlled him.

One day a man buying drugs became angry with me, poured gas on me, and tried to light it. By God's grace, the lighter failed to work, and I survived. John sat there the whole time and did nothing to try to protect or save me.

This was the tipping point. The marriage ended that day. I left him and went back to Arab.

Joy and Pain

I was born into this world to be a happy girl,
But you brought on the pain
each time I tried to love.
You made me think I was insane.

I loved you more than any I knew,
But you tried to kill my love and wouldn't let it grow;
But secretly I loved anyway,
As long as I didn't let it show.

With my love I could make it through the day.
For every beating you gave me, I loved you anyway.
You made me cry and tried to keep me sad,
But every day I awoke my heart was glad.

You tried to teach me to hate like you,
But it wasn't in God's plan.
He gave me a heart full of love,
And that's something you can't understand.

Why am I not like you? I wouldn't want to be, even if I tried.
You wanted to kill my spirit but you released my soul
To love and breathe and breathe and love.
And now I grow and grow and grow.

Being deeply loved by someone gives you strength.
Loving someone deeply gives you courage.

Chapter Twenty

He Became My Baby

Shortly after John was gone, Roy Boyd, my dad, came to Arab to die. No one would take care of him, so I gave up my home and moved in with him and his wife. I could not bear children because of this man, and I hated him for that. But God knew I needed to forgive him before he died, that I needed a healing process, so He put me in this situation for that reason.

The sicker Dad got, the more he became like my baby. I never let him get bed sores or failed to give him his pain medicines. I took care of him with pride but also with pain. I bathed him, changed him, fed him, dressed him, combed his hair, and made his bed every day. I begged my family to give me a break occasionally, but no one would come.

The day he died, however, everyone was there, even my mom. All my life he had denied what he did to me, but that day he said, "Oh God, forgive me for what I've done. Ila, will you forgive me?" I replied, "I've already forgiven you. I wouldn't have come home if that was not true." My mom also asked me to forgive her because she had not believed me over the years.

Dad's deathbed request for forgiveness was not the first during his illness. Every time I tried to leave his bedside, he would beg me to come back and would ask me to forgive him... again and again. He asked if I would stay and take care of his wife Joyce after he was gone, and I did stay with her three years. I have no regrets about the way I took care of him or her.

On the day he died, a Great Pyrenees dog ran in front of my car. To me, this was more than mere coincidence. Dad had often told me how beautiful Great Pyrenees dogs were. He said that if he could be reincarnated, he would want to come back as that breed of dog. When I got home the night of his death and saw that dog on the front porch, I knew my dad was gone.

Five months later, on Father's Day, I was feeling a little depressed. My mom said it was because I had gotten to know Dad better while I was taking care of him. That evening the power went out, so I retreated to the front porch. Standing there was that Great Pyrenees dog. He walked over to me and put his head in my lap. Then he went toward our dog Yeller, and Yeller immediately sat down. (My dad was the only person who could make Yeller sit.) Then, just as suddenly, the dog disappeared.

By the way, two of my sisters also saw the same dog that Father's Day. We've never seen that dog again.

You Couldn't Break Me

Since the day I was born you tried to break my spirits.
I don't know why the more I try to win your love and affection,
the more you want to mistreat me.
You never got to know me. You never wanted to.

I'm Ila.
I'm pretty and sometimes funny.
I'm smart. I like to sing.
I love children, and I write poems.
After all you put me through
I still have compassion,
and that's from God.
You couldn't take love from me.
You couldn't make me hate.

Would it have killed you to give me a hug
or a pat on the head?
But, no, you just wanted to keep me in your bed.
I was not a whore. I was your daughter.
Didn't that mean anything to you?
Did you notice that you emotionally disturbed me?

I forgive you.
In fact, I thank you.

In the Garden (Dirt) – A New Start

I'm in the garden, but I'm not here to plant food.
I'm here to bury the dirt you put on me,
not just inside me but in my mind.

You almost had me convinced that incest was normal,
when in fact it was insurmountable and criminal.
The acts you committed were dirty, just as you are –
I'll never be able to forget the scent of booze and lust
which will always have me in disgust.

So today I rid myself of the heinous acts
you placed upon me starting at age three.
I wash and I wash, but the stench just won't go away;
so I'll write it all down, put it in a box,
and bury it in the garden's ground.

I release myself of this generational curse
you laid on me like a heavy burden.
I will continue on; I will not stop,
and each time you come to hurt me
I'll write it all down, take it to the garden,
and put it in the same box and in the same ground.

This Little Girl

This little girl – too small to fight,
but she tries with all her might.
The big bad man that takes her life –
She thinks of him as a friend in whom she can depend.
Was he her lover? Was he her friend?

No, he was her father, the demon,
which is why I hate him.
So I want the whole wide world to know
a frightened little girl – too scared to hate.
My body fills like dead weight.
Ask me if I'm happy or sad.
If he were dead, I'd be glad.

This little girl – all grown up now,
and Daddy really is dead.
The day he died, this is what he said,
"Oh God, forgive me!
Will You forgive me too, Hon?"

I smile and I know,
for God had also visited me that day.
He said, "Forgive all those who have trespassed against you,
or you will never be able to receive the man
I handpicked just for you."

Chapter Twenty-One

Letting Go

The phone call came from the UAB Hospital intensive care unit in Birmingham. The lady on the other end of the phone said, "You need to come. Your husband is here. He's been badly beaten."

In spite of the pain the man had bestowed on me, I went to see John. I walked into the hospital room and felt no sympathy for him. He could not talk and was paralyzed, so I had to get the details from his friend Ron. He told me that John had been beaten while trying to rob a man.

I told the doctor to send John to Ohio where his family lived. I made it clear he could not come home with me. He was transferred to a nursing home in Ohio for two years. His condition slowly improved there. He began to talk again, but his speech remained slurred. He started walking fairly well and regained use of his arms. He would call me once a week telling that me he loved me and how he had changed, asking for another chance.

So I brought him back to Arab (what was I thinking?), and history repeated itself. In fact, things actually were worse this time. Now he blamed me for his injuries. He told me that he would often lie in bed and think of a thousand ways to kill me without getting caught. To be honest, I thought about filling a syringe with his insulin and shooting it in him, but it just wasn't in me.

I started sleeping on the couch and did so for the next seven years. Sometimes I'd wake up and he'd be standing over me with a knife. I stayed sick a lot, and I began to think that he really was trying to kill me. I had never cheated on him before his injuries and he had been impotent the last seven years, but I was accused of sleeping with everything that walked.

As hard as it may be to believe, John even became jealous of my little Chihuahua, so jealous that he killed him. About a year later he threatened my new puppy. "Get out of here, you little black mutt," he shouted, "before you end up drowned like Pepper Jack." That was all I could stand. I walked in his room, slapped him as hard as I could, packed my stuff, and left him.

Several days later it was real cold outside, and I didn't know if John had any kerosene, so I went to check on him. When I walked into his trailer, it was filled with black soot. The smoke was so thick I could hardly breathe. John was lying unconscious on the couch. I pulled him into the yard and called the paramedics. When they arrived, they called Med-Flight and air-lifted him to Huntsville. I never went to the hospital to see him. I called and told them to send him to a nursing home, and they did.

A few months later I got another call saying that john needed brain surgery and that the doctor would not perform the surgery unless someone was there before John was put to sleep. So once again I went to John. He kept saying, "I know you loved me. Are we going to be together?" I didn't want anything negative on his mind at the time, so I just kept saying, "We'll talk about it when you wake up."

When the doctor came in, I went into the hall and told him everything about John's treatment of me. I made it clear that I was there only because I had to be present for the surgery to happen. I informed him that I was leaving as soon as John was asleep. The doctor replied to me that I was the strongest women he had ever known and that he understood why I would leave.

When I returned to the room, John said, "Baby, if I can't come home with you, I don't want to wake up." Again I replied, "We'll talk about it when you wake up," all the while knowing I'd never have him back.

All this added greatly to my sadness and loneliness. I had reached the bottom. As the psalmist wrote, I was broken-hearted. So I let go and started going to church. Just like the Bible promised, God heard me in my distress.

Good Little Girl in Me

I don't want to leave.
I feel safe here.
But I have to go, so I can grow
into the lady God created me to be.

I've learned so much lately –
forgiveness and trying to trust.
The more I tell myself I'm good, funny, and smart,
I don't believe it anymore.

They don't want me to learn
how to be the best I can be,
Because they like it
when I'm down and depressed.

So goodbye, family and friends.
If you don't believe in me,
This is your notice.
I don't want any more negative in my life.

If you are here to give me
a word of encouragement, thanks;
But I will not allow you
to discourage me any longer.

My Father Said "No"

Why was I ever conceived?
Only God knew.
He must have had a plan for me.

The more I go through, the stronger I get.
The stronger I get, the more I go through.
There's no testimony without a test.

God took my mess
and turned it into a message.
He breathed on me and set me free.

They said I couldn't or I wouldn't,
He said I could and I would.
They said I was nothing.
He said I would sit with the highest of the high.
They said I'd never get clean; I'd always be high.

But He said,
"Smile, My beloved. Trust me. You're really free.
You're here because of Me.
They didn't want you – that much is true,
But I chose you even before you were in your mother's womb.

When bad things came your way, you would cry and say,
'Lord, please let me die!'
That's when I would hold you in My arms
And you would sleep.

They saw you as weak.
I see you as strong.
They always told you that you were wrong,
But I kept holding on.

Whenever they pushed you away,
I stayed right here.
I am your Father.
You, My child, are precious and dear."

Chapter Twenty-Two

The Man God Handpicked for Me

I went to Celebrate Recovery in Arab, where Brother Rick Lassiter was leading the services. That night they played "I Surrender All", and I ran to the altar pouring my heart out to God. I gave Him everything.

I went home, and about midnight some Marshall County deputies burst in looking for a meth lab. I told them they could look, because I knew the house was clean.

One of the officers said, "There's nothing here. Let's go." But the other officer had another plan. "You do meth in Marshall County," he told me, "you go to jail." He then removed a hose from my breathing machine and called it drug paraphernalia.

I went to the county jail and then was transferred to Arab City Jail. I had to stay there thirty days. After twenty days they brought in this handsome, beautiful man. For some reason, I immediately knew that he was the man I dreamed about when I was a little girl.

One day he and I were outside smoking, and we began to confide in each other. He said, "I've had my eyes on you since I got here. I love you."

"You're crazy," I responded. "I can't tell you 'I love you' because I don't know you."

Over the next few days we did get to know each other more. We were allowed to write letters to other inmates, and we would write each other every day. He made me feel confident about myself. When we were together, he would sing songs to me. It was the most beautiful sound I had ever heard. I began to realize that he was mine.

Ten days later I was released and went home, but I came back to pick him up on Monday. We became inseparable. Every day he would build my confidence. He treated me like a lady, something I had never experienced. He opened my car door for me, carried my groceries, and complimented me on everything. He made me feel like I was worth something, that I deserved to be loved. He had to teach me how to trust him in everything.

That was five years ago. I am now in my late forties, and I still love Leron Lockhart with everything that is in me. I am so grateful to Charlie and Grace, his deceased parents, for teaching him how to treat a lady. I have told him *everything* about my past. He is my soulmate, and I thank God for hand-picking him for me.

November 8 was our third wedding anniversary. On our wedding day, Pastor Sterling came and prayed with me before the ceremony. When he saw me, he gasped and told me I was beautiful. He hugged me, and at that moment I felt what I thought it would feel like to get a first hug from your daddy.

Counting dating and marriage, Leron and I have been together for five years, and I could not imagine life without him. It's been over six years since a man last put his hands on me to hurt me. That's an amazing feeling, to wake up and know, whatever happens today, that no one will hurt me. Our marriage, of course, hasn't been a fairy tale. We've had our battles, our ups and downs, but we're still in love with each other. We're also in love with God, and we firmly believe we are still in His plan.

Leron and I go to church together, and our lives have changed since we started doing so. Both of us have been delivered from crack cocaine, and neither of us thinks about getting high. We look at each other with pride. We love each other. We love his family, and they love us. We share a different kind of love than I have ever known. It's Lockhart love, but it's more. It's God's love.

As I look back on my life, I see that God's love has always been with me, even when I didn't realize it. I thank Him for that love each and every day. Without God, I never would have made it.

A Different Love

I was sad and lonely as a little girl.
You told me I was retarded,
I'd never be right in the head,
Then you put me in your bed.

You told me I wasn't worthy of your love,
That I never would comprehend
How a man would never have me.
I'd never have a friend.

But what you didn't know is this –
I'm not retarded and I do comprehend.
I found a man who loves me,
And he is my best friend.

One day I'll marry him
And will live in love till the end.
He'll never beat me or mistreat me.
He loves me just as I am.

Unlike you, he doesn't want to hurt me.
His love is different than yours.
He won't bring me any harm
But will hold me in his arms.

I'm not afraid anymore.
He put me on a pedestal.
He said I was his queen for life
And we would be together.

I am him, and he is me.
He is Leron, my king.

The Love That Taught Me Everything

I never thought I'd feel the magic of your touch,
from being battered and bruised every day of my life,
until I met you.

You had to slow me down.
You told me you wanted to feel my love through my touch
and see it in my eyes.

But I didn't know love.
You taught me everything I know,
how to be loved, how to love and how to relax and trust,
how to make love.

I've never felt this before.
I was forty-six years old when I first felt true love.
I cried, and so did he.

She loves him, and he loves her,
They will be together through eternity.
I am you, and you are me.

Thank you for loving me with real love, not lust.
Thank you for loving me after all the damage he tried to do.
Thank you for helping me heal so we can be complete.

Tears to Laughter

I've cried most of my life because I was lonely.
I had dreamed of true love, but I couldn't find it anywhere.
I looked high and low; I looked everywhere I'd go.

I found many imposters who said they loved me true,
Until they got what they wanted and then they were through,
Leaving me all alone again.

But I kept strong and lingered on until I found him.
I knew he was the one when I looked in his eyes
Through a little hole in the wall.

He made me feel special from day one.
I knew I'd be his darling when he called me "Hon".
His words clung to me.

I knew without a doubt
whatever came out of his mouth was true.
I call him "Boo" and he calls me his "Phoo".
Together we are great.

I know without a doubt he is my soulmate.
He makes me feel complete, like a whole woman.
His love is different.

I thank God for him, my husband and best friend,
He's my hero, my lover, forever near,
The one who brought laughter out of a tear.

How Your Love Feels

I love the way you touch me with your beautiful hands,
the way they glide magically up and down my body,
Feelings I've never had,
leaving me crying in hunger for more.
Each time we touch you take it to another level of ecstasy,
more empowering than anything I've known.

Being beat and battered all my life,
you had to teach me everything,
How to be, how to let go,
so we could go to greater depths with each other,

My man, my best friend, my lover, and my husband –
thank you for being passionate with me.
I am grateful that you decided to marry me.

Then to Now

Now I lay me down to sleep
with tears rolling down my cheek.
I wish I may, I wish I might
sleep with angels tonight.
I wanted to die,
because I was too small to fight,
so I lay there in fright.

Now I'm grown and you are gone,
and I pray to stay,
because you are not worth my life.
I just figured out I'm going to be alright.
I met and married the man
I dreamed would come rescue me.
She loves he and he loves she,
and he will never hurt or mistreat me.
He tells me I'm worth it all
and I can do anything,
and I believe him.

New Attitude

The worst thing that ever happened to me
Is the one thing that made me want to be
A better class of me.
I now have a different kind of attitude.

Can you find gratitude where you hurt?
It's easy to thank God for the good things,
For all the great things He has done.
What about the things that hurt you,
Or the people who hurt you?
Can you find yourself grateful for them?

Can I look up and say,
"God, I want to thank You
For all the things that have happened to me,
For all the people who hurt me"?
For if they had not done what they did,
I wouldn't be here today.

I come before You, God, with gratitude,
With a different kind of attitude –
The mind of Christ.
Thank You for dying for me.

Afterword

I Surrender All (will you?)

I want to say some things to any woman, young or old, who happens to read my story.

- Never give up. God will give you what you need when you need it.
- If you're now going through abuse similar to what I've been through, it's not your fault. Don't let them tell you that it is. It was never your fault.
- Don't be ashamed, and don't hate. Forgive! As long as you hate, they have won; they have beaten you. But when you forgive, they lose all control.
- The choice is yours to trust God and find the courage to live.
- Don't wait until they put roses on your coffin. Surrender everything … now.

I pray that the Lord will bless you as you make your way through life. I pray that His face may shine upon you and that you will be kept in the palm of His hand. I pray that He will be gracious to you and will give you His peace. Amen.

But God

Don't cry for me.
I'm here to tell.

I'm not dead.
I'm not in jail.
I'm not on drugs.
I'm not on the street.

All the times I could have died,
All the times I should have died,
You had me in Your hands.
I was in Your plans.

There is help...

Pastor Keith Hodges – Liberty Church – Arab, Alabama
(256) 931- 4673 or (256) 931-HOPE

Brother Rick Lassiter – Celebrate Recovery – Arab, Alabama
(256) 550-0141

Call 911

Arab Police Department
(256) 586-8124

Marshall Medical Center North
(256) 753-8000

Marshall County Sheriff
256-539-7111

Missing and Exploited Children
(800) THE-LOST

Marshall County Department of Human Resources
(256) 582-7100

Downtown Rescue
(256) 536-2441

There is hope...

Tell a teacher.
Tell a friend.
Tell a stranger.
Just tell someone.

Find a church home.
Volunteer.

Find something to do to occupy your time.

If you just need to feel love, come to
Celebrate Recovery in Arab, Alabama.
It's for any hurt, habit, or hang-up.

You can surrender now.
Pray like you've never prayed before.

There is no pain Jesus cannot fix.
There is no hurt Jesus cannot heal, according to His will.
No matter what you're going through, remember:
God can use you, even in midst of this battle.

Lightning Source UK Ltd.
Milton Keynes UK
UKOW02f0717150117
292090UK00013B/161/P